LITTLE CRITTER
SHAPES

MERCER MAYER

SCHOLASTIC INC.

circle

LITTLE CRITTER®
SHAPES

star

triangle

heart

half circle

oval

square

crescent

diamond

rectangle

my shape

Find the shapes.

No part of this publication may be reproduced, stored in a retrieval system, or transmitted in any form or by any means, electronic, mechanical, photocopying, recording, or otherwise, without written permission of the publisher. For information regarding permission, write to Sterling Publishing Co., Inc., 387 Park Avenue South, New York, NY 10016.

ISBN 978-0-545-84924-1

Copyright © 1992 by Mercer Mayer. All rights reserved.
Published by Scholastic Inc., 557 Broadway, New York, NY 10012, by arrangement with Sterling Publishing Co., Inc. LITTLE CRITTER, MERCER MAYER'S LITTLE CRITTER and MERCER MAYER'S LITTLE CRITTER and logo are registered trademarks of Orchard House Licensing Company. Copyright © 2011 by Mercer Mayer.
SCHOLASTIC and associated logos are trademarks and/or registered trademarks of Scholastic Inc.

12 11 10 9 8 7 6 5 4 3 2   15 16 17 18 19 20/0

Printed in the U.S.A.   40

First Scholastic printing, January 2015

A Big Tuna New Media LLC/ J.R. Sansevere Book